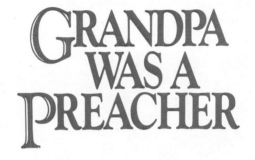

GRANDPA WAS A PREACHER

Presented to:

_____

_____

By:

_____

_____

_____ 19 ____

"Laugh and the world laughs with you."

A Time to Laugh...

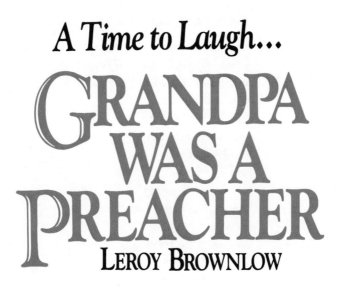

GRANDPA WAS A PREACHER

LEROY BROWNLOW

Brownlow

Brownlow Gift Books

INTRODUCTION

There's "a time to weep, and a time to laugh." Solomon said it. This is Bible.

So — religion is placed on the side of laughter, so much so that the Bible further declares, "A merry heart doeth good like a medicine."

Now is the time to laugh!

And to this end, we present a series of religious anecdotes centering around the life of grandpa who was a preacher. Religion has its funny side, too, for it deals with people. Like the parables of Jesus — earthy, relevant and illustrative — each of these anecdotes teaches a moral principle.

Grandpa didn't have much formal education, but he was way out in front when the brains were passed out and consequently got more than his share. Quick-witted, quick-thinking, he never lacked for an answer. He could rise to any occasion; and when he spoke, he said something.

Grandpa was a giant among men. Like the Homeric heroes — in spiritual and mental measurements — he stood head and shoulders taller than most men. He was prepared for the times, a country preacher fitted to serve a robust people in an evolving society, marked by a mixture of days: good and bad days, sweet and bitter days, moderate and immoderate days, peppery and nonchalant days, lean and fat days, short and long days. But they were his days, the people's days, and he lived them, and he helped others live them.

A society which ached to grow up challenged him with all of its problems; and he met them head-on — giving no quarter and asking no quarter — sometimes with gravity, sometimes with humor, depending upon the circumstances. It was a time of contest — the days tried men and men tried the days.

From the emergence of such struggles, America gained a never-to-be-forgotten heritage. And in the almost complete passing of a breed of men like grandpa, the church, the nation, and the world have suffered an irreparable loss.

Now laugh with us — and learn with us — as we retrace some of grandpa's steps and relive some of his moments. "Laugh and the world laughs with you."

This shrewd man's knack in handling people was most skillful. A big church had a fuss going that was getting hotter and hotter. In an effort to heal the breach and prevent a split, they called in some preachers who gave sharp warnings against division and warm exhortations for unity.

But nobody spoke as briefly (fourteen words) and as effectively as grandpa. Knowing their pride and how they gloried in their size—the largest church in their fellowship—he walked out and in a low-pitched tone said, "You had better get together; for if you split, then you'll be Number Two," and sat down.

It was grandpa's contention that it takes more than a building to make a church. To back it up, he would tell a story to emphasize the point. One day in the city of Eliteville the saloon caught fire, and in the excitement their parrot flew out and down the street where the window was up in Silk Stocking Church and he went in to find his refuge. The next morning the crowd gathered for Sunday worship. The old parrot flew around over the audience a time or two, lighted on the podium and said: "Awk-k-k! The building is different, but it's the same old crowd."

Grandpa believed that many disruptions in life are due to a lack of communication. He went to a boarding school when he was a young man, but he didn't stay long. Through the years his classic explanation for not receiving a formal education was: "The butter was so strong that it stood up and talked to the coffee, and the coffee was too weak to answer — no communication."

Grandpa was a man of justice and mercy. He said: "I study hard to do justice to my sermon and I shut up soon to do mercy to my audience."

This great man of the people recognized that it is not always one's fault when he fails. He used to tell about his going to an irreligious community to hold a revival in which there were no visible results. When asked why his preaching had no effect, he retorted, "Well, I'm not trying to justify myself; nevertheless I think I had the barrel loaded, but they were wearing bullet-proof vests."

Mistaken identity can be perilous. This was grandpa's philosophy. He said that when he first began to preach he was assistant to a caustic elderly preacher, who lived alone, with the exception of a big shaggy dog that had his bed in the kitchen.

Once as grandpa was passing to the kitchen he overheard the old preacher say to a Bible salesman who had just entered the parsonage, "That's my assistant."

The salesman wanted to give a Bible to the parsonage with the understanding that it would be kept on the table in the living room.

"No! No! if you do, that fool back there in the kitchen will just slobber all over it and chew it up," protested the old preacher.

Grandpa said that he tried to get the dog to step to the door and take the characterization; but he was too smart to budge, preferring to let grandpa have the stigma.

This exceptional gospel proclaimer was quick to give a needed lesson. As an aggravated woman, upset by his sermon, was leaving, she said, "I wouldn't like you if you were St. Peter."

"Listen, lady, if I were St. Peter, the only thing that would matter would be whether I liked you," explained grandpa.

As another joke on himself, grandpa would tell the story in which he asked in a children's Bible class, "If I should see a man beating a donkey and stopped him, what virtue would I show?"

A little voice said, "Brotherly love."

Grandpa understood that wealth makes friends. He received a letter from a private college, offering him an honorary doctor's degree.

In his answer he said, "I quickly accept. My only request is that you hurry it up before you learn the rumor is not true: I did not inherit all that money."

"In some places it is best to keep your identity secret," commented grandpa. He said that he went to visit a callused sinner who detested preachers and as he arrived, he was met by a big dog that didn't know whether to be friendly or to attack.

"Do you think that dog will bite me?" asked grandpa.

"Not unless he finds out you're a preacher," responded the belligerent man.

Grandpa was reluctant to recommend threats, but he did in one instance. He had a divorcee to seek his counsel concerning alimony. (That is something one pays for the mistakes of two.) She was afraid her former husband might quit paying, and wanted to know what to do.

Grandpa answered: "Threaten him. Tell him if he doesn't pay, you will repossess him."

In preaching on marriage and divorce, grandpa said, "Some people take the matrimony tie so lightly that to them it is only a forget-me-knot."

"Slow down, if you wish to be caught," was grandpa's philosophy. He went to another town to talk to the church officers who were seeking the services of a new minister. In the meeting, however, he was told, "Parson, we believe the church should seek the man, not the man the church."

"That's one fine way to look at it," replied grandpa, "and just remember when I'm gone that I'll be riding out on the northwest road awfully, awfully slow."

One of the traits of a great man is the disposition to laugh at one's own expense, and grandpa could. He said that in being introduced at his initial service in a revival, a nervous dignitary in a country church said: "A worse preacher would have done us, if we had only knowed where to find him."

Another one grandpa would tell on himself was: "One Sunday my brother, a physician, visited the service. A lady said to him, 'Sir, do you preach, too?' 'No,' was the reply, 'my brother preaches; I practice.'"

Grandpa stated that he reared his children through the trial and error method, and when he erred he tried something else. When his little daughter stumped her toe and said, "Darn!" he reasoned with her: "Sweet, if you'll never say that word again, I'll give you a dime."

A few days later she came to him and said, "Papa, I've got a word now that's worth half a dollar."

"Specialize," was a motto of the parson. An unmarried woman who went with lots of men and loved all of them consulted grandpa because she was still single.

He advised: "Leave loving all men to God. You specialize."

Sometimes grandpa's afterthought was much more efficacious than the primary one. On the official board there was a doctor who was a strictly business, all appointment, short session fellow.

Time was running out in a meeting, but grandpa told a humorous story that had a lesson they needed. All laughed but the doctor who never cracked a smile, because he was just a little irritated at the extension of the time. Then grandpa remarked, ''Doc can never see a joke except by appointment.''

"When you deal with something, don't mince words," was the view of this unusual preacher.

At a preachers' conference that was held to discuss the merits of preaching on hell, the chairman pointed him out and asked, ''Do you preach on hell very often?''

''No, not often.''

''Why not?'' inquired the chairman. ''Is it because you feel that you are not effective on this topic?''

''No, because it disrupts the service.''

''How's that?'' continued the chairman.

''It's like this,'' explained grandpa, ''the audience becomes so fatigued fanning that I have to declare a recess about every five minutes.''

There were times when grandpa used short speeches to great effect. Evolution was beginning to trouble the church — some for it, some against it. A meeting of preachers was called in a distant (100 miles) city to consider the topic. Grandpa was invited to attend and speak. He was last on the program.

Mounting the platform in his country way, he addressed them: "Fellow-preachers, it is getting late, very late. Much has been said, maybe too much. I don't know of anything I can say that will add to it. So I'm going to walk out of here, walk down the street and get a hotel room. Now there's not but one question for the rest of you to decide: Are you going to get a room or a tree?"

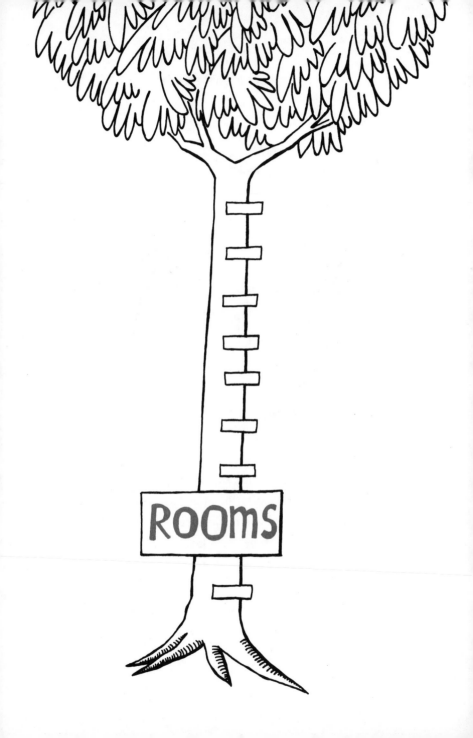

"License to do one thing does not grant permission to do something else," asserted grandpa. For instance: A couple appeared before him, handed him a license, and he married them. As they were leaving, he looked at the instrument and saw it was a hunting license. Running out the door, he yelled, "Hold on! Hold on!" As he handed the license to the man he quipped, "You don't have my permission. I thought you wanted to marry her — not shoot her."

Grandpa was aware that little children consider any person forty awfully old and decrepit. In his older years he visited in a home in which a little boy asked, "Were you in the ark?"

"No, I wasn't," answered the preacher.

"Then why didn't you drown?" inquired the little boy.

Later as grandpa was leaving, he said that he heard a terrible scream which caused him to suspect that the father had put the boy through an aging process pretty fast.

"You shouldn't expect much for nearly nothing," preached grandpa. He said that a family, upon returning home from church, began their devastating criticisms. The mother objected to the sermon. The father ridiculed the ushers. The older sister made light of the singing. But it was little Eddie that tore them up when he said, "Still it was a pretty good show for a dime."

"Tell the truth, but be diplomatic," was another one of grandpa's guiding principles.

In opposing a school tax, an old gentleman went into a tirade: "I know I'm ignorant and I just hope I get ignoranter; for I'm thankful for being ignorant."

Grandpa, giving him a gentle pat on the shoulder and in a tone as sweet as honey, remarked: "Brother, you've got a lot for which to be thankful."

Grandpa said that you can't agree with some men without angering them. One of his cases in point was the agnostic whom he defined as "a man who loudly declares that he knows nothing and abuses you if you believe him."

Grandpa declared, "The sounds which come from an empty head will reveal its hollowness." After delivering a sermon, grandpa was approached by an "educated" visitor who wanted to correct his language. He began: "You used the phrase 'aching void.' I wish you would tell me how a void can ache."

"Well, not to speak of a hollow tooth, don't you sometimes have the headache?" was grandpa's silencer.

The motive for doing a thing was as important to grandpa as the act itself. He said that one day he went to visit an oldster in the country. Grandpa, surprised at finding the man sitting on the porch reading the Bible, commented: "I'm delighted to find you reading the Bible."

"I wuz just lookin' in the Book of Job to see if it tells what he done for boils," was the reply.

Many who stay out of the church give hypocritical excuses instead of reasons for it. A crusty old fellow cornered the preacher on the street and blurted, "Parson, I want you to know the reason I'm not in your church—there are hypocrites in it."

This country sage patted him on the shoulder and said, "That's all right; come on in, there's room for one more."

Grandpa was quick to see potentials. Wanting to buy some land, he went to see a little farm that backed up against a river. He noticed a ring of mud about shoulder high on the trees; so he asked, "Does the river overflow?" "No, no," replied the farmer, "we ain't had no high water in thirty years."

"Then how did that mud get up there?" asked the preacher.

"Oh, that—that was caused by them hogs of mine. They're always rubbing against the trees." After a moment, he asked, "Do you aim to buy the place?"

"No, but I really would like to buy a start of those hogs," answered grandpa.

The parson knew how to make a comparison. A politician who promised everybody everything for nothing was running against a more conservative man. Some sought grandpa's appraisal. He replied, "I try to stay out of politics; but when a man puts himself up greater than Jesus Christ, I guess I ought to say something. Jesus said, 'Follow me and ye shall not want.' But one of the candidates is saying, 'Sit down, fellows, and I'll hand it to you.' "

Grandpa believed that church life demanded reformation. He said, "One winter we broke the ice on an open pond to baptize some people.

" 'Is the water cold, Sam?' asked a deacon of a shivering, dripping convert.

" 'No, not a bit cold,' replied Sam.

" 'Better put him under again, parson,' suggested the deacon, 'he hasn't quit lying yet.' "

"Don't fizzle out on the punch line," advised grandpa in addressing some preachers. He had a humorous story to illuminate the thought. He said that they had a young preacher from the seminary one Sunday, who had heard an older preacher say, "The happiest days of my life were spent in the arms of another man's wife — my mother."

The young preacher thought the quotation would add drama and force to his sermon; so he tried it. "The happiest days of my life were spent in the arms of another man's wife —." At this point he had a mental block; bewildered, he agonized for a moment and said, "To save my life I can't remember who it was."

"Your intentions can be misunderstood," declared grandpa. At a ministers' conference that was long and unproductive he sat for four hours and then arose for the first time.

"The chairman recognizes the standing minister," announced the moderator.

Turning to the chairman, grandpa said, "Brother chairman, I'm not standing for recognition — I'm standing for recreation."

"You don't have the children fooled," was something grandpa often witnessed. He said that in one of his ministerial calls, the whole family gathered around. The conversation drifted into child training, discipline, and awards. The mother impulsively said, "You know, preacher, I'm going to keep a record of the conduct of each for the week and on Saturday I'm going to give a prize to the most obedient one."

"That's not fair!" exclaimed a little boy. "Daddy will win it every week."

Grandpa's advice rang with originality. He was consulted in a very novel case. A young man, fascinated by a young lady, serenaded her outside her window. Being unacceptable to her, she threw a flower pot out the window which creased his head. Outraged, he called on grandpa, whose comment was, "Young man, when you make an uninvited appearance, you should always expect POT LUCK."

Even grandpa knew there were occasions that might prompt strong outbursts of disapproval that would seem tolerable. As he sat at a banquet, a waitress spilled a hot bowl of soup down his neck. He jumped, suffered, held his anger, and finally came out with: "Now's the time for some of you sinners to say something appropriate."

Grandpa never lacked for a rejoinder. In a preachers' luncheon a preacher told them that he dreamed he had gone to heaven and looked and looked and grandpa was not there.

They laughed.

Then it was grandpa's time to reply, and he said, "You know, that's funny, Jim, I had a dream last night, too. I dreamed I went to heaven and the Lord gave me a piece of chalk and said, 'Go over there and write down all your sins.' And just at that time I met you leaving. I said, 'Joe, what are you doing? Why are you going that way?' And you said, 'I'm going to get some more chalk!' "

And they roared.

Since Grandpa had only a little formal education, he enjoyed ribbing the college people. Because of his uniqueness, he was invited to speak at a large college gathering. He congratulated the institution on its vast storehouse of knowledge, and told them he had figured out how they had collected so much. He said, "From my observation, this laudable accomplishment has been achieved because the freshmen bring in so much learning and the seniors take out so little."

The preacher noted that there was a deep concern in the church for the people in their little town, but that it did not extend to others. He said that one Sunday in a Bible class a good sister inquired, "What's this I hear about somebody dropping dead in town yesterday?"

"Yep, sure did. Happened right outside Jim Anderson's Barber Shop," replied an elderly brother, "and for a little while everybody was awfully torn up, but it wasn't so bad — just a summer visitor."

Grandpa believed church members should be thoughtful of their minister, but he thought one woman overdid it. This woman, who took ill suddenly, requested grandpa to come. He was puzzled because she was so active and partisan in another religion. On the way back to her room, he began to talk to the little daughter. He asked, "Is your preacher out of town?"

"Oh no," she answered, "mamma thought she might have something contagious, and she just couldn't take any chances with him."

"You can make a good case out of nothing, if you disregard evidence," was some of grandpa's preaching.

It was the day of Model T Fords. Many who had them knew nothing about operating them and consequently had their vexing problems. An irate dairyman who was finding his Tin Lizzie hard to crank complained to the preacher that the difficulty was due to a dishonest filling station operator who was selling watered gasoline.

Grandpa reasoned with him: "Now, Sam, you don't have any proof of that. Furthermore, this morning I saw you water the cows before you milked them."

Gossip is one of the most disruptive sins in society. Grandpa had one of the flock to complain about the inattention of another member. She said, "When you talk to her, it just goes in at one ear and out at the other. Can you think of anything as bad as that?"

"Yes, if it went in at one ear and out at the mouth," answered the preacher.

Grandpa's ability and freeness to josh himself before a congregation endeared him to them. In the middle of a sermon at a new place, a member tiptoed up toward the pulpit, taking grandpa a glass of water. But he waved him away, saying, "I don't drink when I'm talking. I can't run a windmill on water."

The sage from the hills excelled in diplomatic but effective rebukes. He was the chairman of a committee on a civic improvement project. One of the committeemen was inclined to profanity. Not wanting to shame him grandpa remained silent. But enough was enough, so he decided to act. At the next meeting the parson said, "Mr. Jones, before we discuss the question, we assume that everybody and everything is damned; so now we can proceed with the discussion respectfully."

Grandpa regretted that some people separated thinking from speaking. He was invited to address the state legislature. They liked his quips. Among them, he told that as he arrived at a political meeting the month before he asked Jim Jones, one of the legislators, "What do you think about a tax increase?"

"Don't ask me what I think," replied Jones, "I've got to make a speech, and that's no time to think."

Grandpa knew how to whistle for what he wanted. A rich man had held up giving what he pledged on the building fund, telling everybody that he was not going to give it until the preacher whistled for it — but grandpa was determined not to ask him. Time passed and no payment, then one Sunday grandpa announced to the congregation a slight change in the services:

"When you get to the last stanza of the song I want you to refrain from singing the chorus, for I shall whistle it." And as he did, he looked over to the slow giver and winked.

Grandpa learned that most people have abilities they don't realize. And this is one of his examples:

"An irate sheep (or goat) in the flock came to grandpa, wanting help in framing a letter to a neighbor about a fence and some cattle. He said, "I ain't got larnin' enough to express myself."

"What do you want to say to him?" queried grandpa as he picked up the pen.

"Well," answered the farmer, "you can first begin by calling him the meanest, thievinest, lyinest, lowdownest, stinkinest skunk on earth, and then work up to something hard."

Grandpa was thoughtful. He went to the hospital one night to see a sinner friend he had not been able to reach. The man, beginning to rally from surgery, asked, "Why are the shades pulled?"

The preacher answered, "I asked the nurse to do that, Tom. You see, there's a fire across the street, and I didn't want you to think the operation had been a failure."

Grandpa was an understanding man, because he lived close to the people. He knew them and their problems. One Sunday he publicly called on a farmer to lead prayer. This straightforward man of the soil refused, saying, "Pardon me, please, I've been breaking young mules all week."

"Having people in debt to you makes enemies," was some more of the country preacher's philosophy. It was told him that one of his old friends was saying some nasty things about him. He then leaned back and in a spirit of reflection said, "That's strange. I don't recall ever lending him any money."

Grandpa learned that it was easy for people to hear in his preaching what they wanted to hear. In speaking to one of the alcoholic characters in the flock, he said, "Jim, whiskey is your worst enemy."

"Well, preacher," he responded, "you told us in the pulpit only last Sunday to love our enemies."

"So I did," rejoined grandpa, "but I didn't even get close to telling you to swallow them."

"It won't do any good to knock down the cobwebs unless you kill the spider!" This was another piece of grandpa's philosophy.

A man who always prayed the same prayer word for word was leading the congregation. They could go three words ahead of him all the way through. Part of it went like this: "Oh Lord, since we last called upon thee, the cobwebs have come between us and thee. We pray that thou wilt remove the cobwebs that we may look upon thy face once again."

Just at this point, grandpa spoke a little louder than he intended, "Oh Lord, kill the spider."

"Some people are just too slow to ever get anything done," was one of the comments of this extraordinary preacher. This was exemplified in one of his funerals.

From the cemetery the director drove the lonely widow —all alone— in the family car back to her home. On the way, he said, "Mary, I don't want you to think I'm too forward or this is too soon, but all my life I've been too slow; and I don't want it to happen in this case; so if you should ever anticipate another marriage, I wish you would think of me."

She replied, "I appreciate that very much, Henry, but the doctor has already asked me."

Grandpa believed human nature has been the same all along. At a town hall meeting a famous lecturer discussed domestic affairs. In the speech he said, "What would Eve have done if Adam had come home late at night?"

Silence prevailed.

Then he said, "I understand a preacher is in the audience. I shall ask him: What would Eve have done if Adam had come home late at night?"

"She would have counted his ribs," answered grandpa.

It was grandpa's philosophy that our troubles are due to man — not nature's vicissitudes. And this thought extemporaneously came out in one of his sermons in which he said, "Man's hardships are not due to the apple on the tree, but to the *pair* on the ground."

Grandpa's wit and forthrightness enabled him to handle the mischief-makers. He held a revival in a community where some profane men decided to break up his meeting. In his first sermon, one of the men stood up and commanded, "Louder!" Accordingly, grandpa raised his voice. A little later the man stood and said again, "Louder!" And louder grandpa got until surely everybody could hear. But shortly the man stood again and roared, "Louder!"

It was then that grandpa stopped his sermon and said, "Ladies and gentlemen, the day will come when this old world will quit turning, the sun will cease to shine, the stars will fall and explode, and Gabriel will blow the trumpet so loud that it will be heard around the world; and at that time I'm sure one in this crowd will stand up and holler, 'Louder!' "

It was grandpa's philosophy that there can be too much of a good thing. A young preacher was scheduled to give a special sermon at the evening hour, but in the afternoon he began to get hoarse. He asked grandpa what to do to relieve it.

Grandpa advised: "Get some brandy and pour a little in a glass and fill the rest of the glass with water. Take it into the pulpit and as you preach, just sip it a little at intervals and your voice will clear up."

After the sermon was concluded, the young preacher asked grandpa how he liked it.

"Well, in all candor, I didn't."

"You didn't? Why didn't you?"

Then grandpa answered: "I have my reasons. In the first place, I didn't say put a cherry in it. Secondly, I said sip it — not gulp it. Thirdly, the Sermon on the Mt. was not preached in New York City. Fourthly, there are Ten Commandments — not fourteen. And in the fifth place, when David killed the giant Goliath he used a sling and a stone — he didn't stomp his insides out."

Grandpa believed that he who laughs last laughs best.
He and the minister of another church were walking
together one frosty day when grandpa slipped and fell flat
on his back. Seeing that he wasn't hurt, the other preacher
laughed and said, "Friend, sinners stand on slippery
places."

Grandpa looked up as if to assure himself of the fact,
and said, "I see they do, but I can't."

Our great man of the people wasn't much for self-laudation disguised as testimonials. He visited a service in which many took turns at testifying about how much they were doing for the Lord. Then the presiding preacher called on grandpa to tell them all what he was doing for the Cause.

Grandpa stood, looked around and said, "When a man's work is speaking for itself, I prefer not to interrupt," and sat down.

It was grandpa's viewpoint that every man is multi-colored, depending on circumstances; so why argue about color? But not everybody shared his views. Thus a religious conference was held to discuss the color line. Some spoke for segregation, others for integration. Grandpa, toward the last of the program, in his characteristic way, said, "When a man is white, he is scared; when he is yellow, he is sick; when he is red, he is embarrassed; and when he is black and blue, he has just had an argument with his wife. So why get worked up about color?" He then sat down.

This sufficed. For they saw that color is something more than skin deep.

"Stingy members often block progress on the grounds that a church doesn't need a certain thing," was an observation of the discerning preacher. He wanted to build a multi-purpose building close to the other building.

When opposition began to show, he decided to visit the opposers. One was a dry goods merchant, who immediately said, "Now, parson, you're trying to sell us something we don't need. Our church doesn't need two buildings."

Grandpa rejoined, "Now, Henry, if your principle is right, then you're the champion seller of things not needed. I stood right here in this store last week and saw you sell two hats to a man with only one head."

The parson believed in giving responsibilities to children early and increasing them with age. This was seen in an appearance before a ladies' group in a question and answer session.

A perturbed mother said, "Preacher, what do you do to get a teenage daughter out of hot water?"

"Try putting some dishes in it," was his practical answer.

Here is one that always made grandma blush, and grandpa enjoyed telling it. In counseling a very bumptious man, he said, "You should develop more humility. There is One before whom I am only a crawling worm. Do you know who?"

"Sure," replied the fellow, "the missus."

Grandpa knew that no man in public life should undervalue the women. A reporter for a woman's magazine came to town and contacted him for some leads. She inquired, "Do you know any professional women?"

"Well, I've never met an amateur one," was his true appraisal.

Grandpa believed that women should be discreet. And in a discussion of the topic he stated in his sermon, "As I was walking down the street a young lady in the church was accosted by a sailor who said, "Want to go with me, baby?"

"Guess how she handled it?" inquired grandpa. "She replied, 'Listen here, a public street is no place to speak to a strange, nice girl who lives at 433 Pine St., whose phone is 27886.' "

Grandpa knew the penalty for over-indulgence. At a Sunday church dinner the members enjoyed making sport of his eating so much (though he didn't). One man said, "Parson, if you eat any more, you'll burst."

Grandpa replied, "Listen, everybody: pass the cake, and stand back."

The best conduct can have its exceptions. A visitor inquired of the preacher, "I suppose these people are always kind, polite, and sweet spirited?"

"Well, most of the time. Maybe there's only one exception."

"How's that?"

"Just try getting in their pew," was his answer.

Grandpa recognized that there could be only one alternative in some cases. He went home with a family for Sunday dinner. They had everything to eat and lots of it. Furthermore, they needed it, for the gluttonous father was a champion eater.

"I see you enjoy your eating," suggested grandpa.

"Not especially," answered the old man.

"Now, I get it — you are just uncontrollably fond of bicarbonate of soda," commented grandpa.

This original preacher was strong for vicarious suffering. On a preaching tour he spent the night with a farm family that had bed bugs. After clawing and scratching the most of the night, he finally killed one. He stuck a pin through it and a piece of paper which he pinned to the wall. The note on the paper read, "He died that I might live."

Grandpa believed that the man who dishes it out ought to be able to take it. And he could. And with an equal amount of fun.

In one of his sermons he compared the preacher to a shepherd and the members to sheep. Then he asked, "What does the shepherd do for the sheep?"

To the uncontrollable amusement of the audience, a little boy on the front row answered, "Shears them!" It shocked grandpa for a moment and, getting hold of himself, he said, "Then let's bring in some more sheep."

Grandpa believed in occasionally using the shock treatment. In a church business meeting, he proposed that they bring in some ballet dancers.

They were horrified! simply horrified! and asked for an explanation.

With a twinkle in his eye, he replied, "For one time, for just one time, I would like to see some people in this church on their toes."

Grandpa was strong on practicality. As a young minister, he preached a trial sermon in a village church, hoping to be called to that pulpit. Later the officials met with him to question his abilities. Wanting to be sure they got an educated man, they, with the help of a school teacher, had worked up a few special questions to test him.

The lead man, with an air of scholarship, began: "Preacher, would you say a hen sets or sits?"

The young sage from the hills answered: "I don't care ~ther she sits or sets. What I'm interested in is: When ~'les, is she laying or lying?"

~ no more questions. He got the job.

It was grandpa's view that man often takes credit when credit is not due. He said that at the conclusion of a service he spoke to a stranger: "I observed the close attention you gave my sermon. Your upturned face was an inspiration to me. I am sure you never changed your earnest attitude during my sermon."

"No," said the man, "I have a stiff neck."

Grandpa took sunshine to the sufferer. While visiting an old man afflicted with rheumatism, he was asked the question: "Preacher, could there be any physical ailment worse than inflammatory rheumatism?"

"Yes, rheumatism and St. Vitus's dance both at the same time would be worse."

A good laugh and the man who was losing courage regained it and felt better.

Grandpa knew the cheapest way to get things done. He said, "There is no need to pay to have your family tree traced — just run for office and it will be done free."

Grandpa asserted that it was quite an accomplishment for a minister just to wake up some people at church. One Sunday the town idler and drunk staggered into worship. Grandpa was preaching on sin. Wanting to impress upon his audience the awfulness of the topic, he stopped and asked, "What is it that is so easy to get into and so hard to get out of?"

There was a silence for a moment and then the sleepy winebibber said, "Bed."

Like lightning, grandpa grabbed back his audience by saying, "I've done pretty well today just to wake up Bill."

Grandpa had a deep insight to the design of the commandments. He always thought he knew why the Lord had taught that adults must be converted and become as little children — because the child's innocence causes him to put the best construction on everything, even that which seems most unlikely.

He said that as he was walking to town, a little girl ran out and told him about her father: "You ought to be proud of my papa. I bet he's the religionest man in the church. This morning when he hit his thumb with the hammer, he jumped up and down and talked about God for fifteen minutes."

"Any good thing can be overdone," insisted grandpa. To illustrate, he said that during a visit with a shiftless fellow he inquired, "Have you been sleeping well lately?"

"Not the best in the world. I sleep real good nights, purty good mornin's; but afternoon, I jest toss and tumble," complained the idler.

Grandpa could laugh at himself, which is one of the tests of a great man. He said he sent this order to a mail house: "Please send me one of the lanterns you show on page 148; and if it's any good, I'll send you a check."

He said a few days later he received the following reply: "You send the check; and if it's any good, we'll send the lantern."

Grandpa had a practical explanation as to why mature women look older than mature men. He said, "It is because a mature woman of 39 is generally 50."

Grandpa believed that every man should understand the real source of his calling. After hearing a young man preach his maiden sermon which was such a pathetic failure, the members wondered how the young preacher could do so poorly if he had been called.

"Maybe it was a local call instead of long distance," retorted the country preacher.

"There is power in suggestion," philosophized grandpa. And he used it to good purpose. They had a revivalist who was preaching extra long sermons and the people were complaining. About half way through the revival, he preached, "There Is a Sermon in Every Blade of Grass."

The next morning, accompanied by the visitor, grandpa got the mower out to mow the grass.

"Why are you mowing? Why don't you let the yard man do it?" inquired the revivalist.

"I just wanted to show you how to cut the sermons shorter," rejoined grandpa.

"Some people's clarification is compounded confusion," insisted grandpa. He said that a young preacher from the seminary, visiting with them, introduced his sermon by stating: "I shall speak on 'Epitomes of the Life of Paul.' Perhaps some do not grasp the meaning of 'epitomes'; therefore, I should clarify it, and thus without multiplicity of verbosity or unnecessary circumlocution, I would say that it is in its signification synonymous with synopsis."

"There is no need to travel unless you know your direction," was one of grandpa's mottoes. He said that one Sunday they had a guest speaker, a student from a seminary. After the service, grandpa overheard him ask one of the deacons, a grizzled, plain-spoken man, what he thought of the morning's efforts.

"Waal," answered the old man slowly, "I'll tell ye; I'll tell ye in a kind o' parable. It reminded me of Sim Peck's furst deer hunt when he was green. He follered the deer's tracks all right, but he follered 'em all day in the wrong direction."

"There is no gain in being owed what can't be collected," reasoned grandpa. When the officers of the church increased his salary, he went before the flock and said: "I beg you not to increase my pay; for it is just about as time-consuming as I can afford to collect my present salary; and if it should be increased, I might have to devote so much time to rounding it up that I wouldn't have time for anything else."

Grandpa learned that many people are satisfied to have just a little bit of Bible in their homes. In one of his house calls he asked for their Bible, wanting to read a passage. Then they called in the children and organized a hunt for the Good Book. At last one of the children dug up a few wrinkled pages of Holy Scripture. The father took the pages and triumphantly handed them to the preacher.

"This is no Bible," protested grandpa.

The man argued, "Yes, it is, but I didn't know we were so nearly out."

It was grandpa's view that it is wise to find out what a person is seeking. He said that while he was preaching one Sunday a tall, lean, country boy walked in and stood at the back.

Grandpa stopped his sermon and inquired, "Young man, are you seeking salvation?"

He replied, "No, I'm seeking Sal Johnson. Is she here?"

"It is always heartening to be reassured," asserted grandpa. And he stated that such came from a visiting revivalist, who preached in his sermon on future punishment, "Yes, beloved brethren, there is a hell —" (pulling out his watch and looking at it) "but we shall not go into it just now."

This Bible proclaimer believed in keeping rudeness to a minimum. The speaker at a preacher's meeting kept needling the group until grandpa finally whispered to the preacher beside him.

The speaker stopped and interjected the statement, "It's rude to whisper when another is speaking."

"Yes, but it would have been a lot ruder to say it out loud," replied the country parson.

━━━━━━━━━━

"You should not do unto others without their consent," was another principle taught by grandpa. And sometimes the lesson was most telling. He went to the new barber for a haircut. After changing the style and peeling him, the barber held the mirror behind grandpa's head and inquired, "Is that O.K.?"

"Well, not quite, just a little longer in the back, please," was the revolting but needful answer.

━━━━━━━━━━

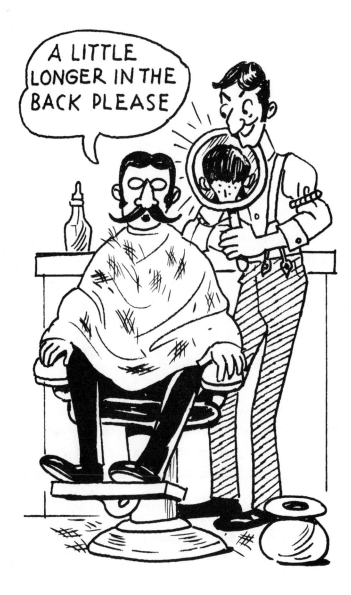

"It's never wise to lift up one person by knocking another down," voiced this country sage. He said that as he stood at the back of the church, he overheard one man ask another, "Who is that ugly woman over there?"

"That's my wife," was the sharp reply.

The inquirer blushed, coughed, and finally uttered, "Well, you just ought to see mine."

Grandpa believed in child discipline. For instance, in a question and answer period concerning child training, he was asked, "Don't you think we need much more training at mother's knee?"

"Yes, and sometimes a little over father's knee," was his advice.

"Sometimes courtesy keeps one from using the right word," stated grandpa. A distraught brother who had critical financial problems called on him. After listening for a while to his plight, the preacher said, "Would you say your troubles are due to mismanagement?"

"My wife manages the money," replied the caller.

"Oh, I see," answered grandpa. "It's not mismanagement — it's Mrs. Management."

Grandpa had a reason for seeing some and refusing others. During a period of illness in which he was denying himself the presence of all visitors, he received a well-known infidel. The atheist said, "I appreciate this, but why do you receive me when you refuse your church friends?"

"Well, it's like this," said grandpa. "I expect to see my believing friends in the next world, but this may be the last time I'll see you."

"Live up to your doctrine," was often mentioned by grandpa. But this principle took an unseemly turn of events while he was discussing religious topics with an unschooled member of the flock. The member stated that the best of people are none too good.

"Oh, you believe in the doctrine of total depravity," injected grandpa.

"Yep, sure do," responded the member, "that is, — er, — er when it's lived up to."

A big city preacher requested grandpa to give him a statement of commendation for his new book. Grandpa hated to decline, but had to on the grounds that it was not exactly in keeping with his views.

The author replied, "You can't appreciate it, because you never wrote a book."

"No," retorted the country preacher, "and neither have I ever laid an egg, but I think I'm a better judge of an omelet than any hen in the world."

This preacher-philosopher was never impressed with numbers like he was with quality. A state representative returned home from a recent session of the legislature and began to strut and brag about their successes. While caught up in this spirit of accomplishment, he met grandpa on the street and stated, "We've just passed seventy-nine laws in three months, how many have you at the church passed?"

In his forceful, subdued manner, the parson responded, "Well, lawyer, you're doing better than God, he gave only TEN."

Grandpa was more understanding of women who misrepresent their age than most people. He rather justified their loose way of stating their age. He said, "The years they knock off before sixty they will add on after eighty."

This self-made man could rise to any occasion. In one of his revivals, some young "toughs" decided to so harass him that he would pack up and leave. After grandpa got into his sermon, one of them stood up and asked: "What's the difference between a preacher and a fool?"

"Stand here beside me a moment and I think the audience can see the difference," was the shocking answer.

But they were still determined, not knowing how calamitous it was to go against grandpa. So the next morning as he walked to the post office, three of them were stationed along the way. As he approached, one of them jerked off his hat, bowed and said, "Good morning, father Abraham." The second made the same gesture and said, "Good morning, father Isaac." The third one tipped his hat, bowed low and spoke, "Good morning, father Jacob."

Grandpa stopped, turned and stated: "I am neither Abraham, Isaac nor Jacob. I am Saul, the son of Kish, out seeking my father's asses, and I've just found three of them."

> Purposing to improve his voice, Ass went
> And listened to the songsters in the dale —
> Blackbird, lark, nightingale.
> "I'm better than them all!" he thought and sent
> His loudest phrases through the startled trees:
> "Have you notes such as these
> For drama, volume, power?"
> Horror held the songsters dumb. Ass strode away
> Triumphant to his bower,
> Having silenced every rival with his bray.
> — Mark Heim

But not grandpa! He silenced them instead.

Grandpa had an answer for the flimflamers. For instance: A high powered salesman called on him. The pressure man was determined to sell him a book on communications. He said, "You can study this, learn just a few effective words, and get rich like I have."

The parson, seeing the peddler was a fraud, answered, "Words like, 'Stick 'em up?' "

Grandpa believed preachers should do more than talk — say something. A sophisticated lady said to him, "Don't you think Dr. Flowery makes charming Lenten addresses?"

From him the truth spontaneously flowed "Yes, and they are so appropriate, too — there's so little meat in them."

Grandpa knew that an internal conflict would often cause a compromise. Some disturbed women called on him in his study. Their concern was short skirts — already half way to the knee.

One inquired, "Brother, why will they do that?"

"Well, maybe they are caught in the struggle between the yielded urge to dress and the unyielded urge to undress," was his answer.

"Misfortune for one may be fortune for another," declared grandpa. His son, Johnny, was the first in the little town to take the measles. The doctor never sent grandpa a bill. Later when the doctor attended the services, which he seldom did, grandpa explained: "I want to publicly thank the doctor for attending Johnny when he had the measles, and most of all for not sending me a bill. This I can't figure out unless it's because Johnny infected the whole school for him."

Grandpa stated that some people are so negative that they are against everything, even the good. While getting acquainted with the people in a new congregation, he met an old man who said that he had been a member there for sixty-five years.

"I guess you've seen some mighty big changes here, haven't you?" inquired grandpa.

"Yep, sure have, and I've been against all of them," answered the old man.

This Bible proclaimer believed that selfishness is the root of most unhappiness. He was once asked if he had ever performed an unhappy marriage.

"Yes," he answered, "the bride wept for two hours. I don't know, but it could have been the groom got a bigger piece of cake than she did."

In one of grandpa's revivals under a brush arbor, there were some young men who plotted to break up the meeting. Unacquainted with grandpa's wit, one of them stood in the middle of the sermon and asked him a question. After answering the question, grandpa asked him one. Not hearing a reply, the parson asked, "Why don't you answer my question?"

The confounded querist said, "I did. I shook my head."

"You don't expect me to hear the rattle way up here, do you?" rejoined grandpa.

Experience taught the parson that you need to be prepared for anything when you ask a question, especially in the presence of children. A couple, wishing to be married, came accompanied by a large group to the parsonage. In getting the participants to stand before him properly, he asked, "Who is the best man?"

"That's the one who doesn't get the bride," blurted out the groom's little brother.

"If you don't know the answer, at least try to be practical," suggested the clever preacher.

At the end of the sermon, he threw the service open for questions. As usual, this one was asked, "Where did Cain get his wife?"

Grandpa answered: "I'm glad you asked that. Now let me give you a little advice. Don't lose your soul salvation inquiring about another man's wife.

Knowing what to say gave this country parson extraordinary power. For instance: In keeping with their prearranged plan, some disgruntled college students began walking out when grandpa was about half way through a chapel speech.

"Don't go just now," pleaded the parson, "I have a few more pearls to cast."

"Some people's encouragement can be most discouraging," reasoned grandpa. And he had an experience to prove it. Caught up in the spirit of his sermon, he went way over time. When he realized it, he apologized and closed.

Then a lady rushed up and offered her consolation: "Preacher, you didn't talk long — it just seemed long."

Grandpa knew how to bring a proposition to a focal point. The finance committee, wanting to raise some extra money for a special project, asked him to speak on giving just prior to taking up the collection. Well, this country preacher made a very forceful plea and concluded by saying: "Judge yourselves. Christians give and heathen receive; so everybody put in something or take out something."

This man of homespun philosophy believed that back-bone and grit will make you a winner. He had a very satisfactory explanation of why the lions didn't eat Daniel — "because the most of him was backbone and the rest was grit."

It was grandpa's view that there is a difference between education and intellectualism. He insisted that intellectualism is the ability to think, while educaton is learning another's thinking, which he said is often no more than "parrotism — with notes." He contended that the market is a place to go and buy brains — not a college; and that the best any college can do is to polish the ones you already have.

Grandpa was a friend of the outcast and the downtrodden. One such a man had a case in court and grandpa testified in his behalf. While in the witness chair, the opposing attorney began to belittle him, calling him a "corn-field preacher." This he didn't mind until the lawyer began to slur religion, and it was then that grandpa decided to teach him to have more respect.

The attorney, sticking both hands in his pockets and leaning backward in a pose of lordship, said, "Preacher, aren't you a little out of character here in court?"

Like a flash, grandpa replied, "Aren't you as a lawyer a little out of character, too, standing there with your hands in your own pockets?"

It nearly broke up the court; furthermore, the lawyer was almost hurrahed out of town.

Grandpa knew there was a difference between sound and sanity. In going through a city church, he came to something he didn't understand. The city preacher explained: "That's a sounding board, something to throw out the sound."

"Oh, you must be pretty good," commented grandpa, "for I know a scad of preachers who couldn't use that and have anything left."

It's easy to say what you would do if you were in the other fellow's place when you don't know the place he's in," stated this perceptive preacher.

To illustrate he would tell a true story of himself and a brother in the church who went walking in a pasture. For protection against deer hunters they wore red jackets. In time a bull spotted them and gave chase. They ran until finally the brother grabbed a limb and went up a tree, while grandpa darted into a little cave. But no sooner had he gotten in until he darted out. And then the bull charged and away grandpa flew back into the cave. And it became a bullet-like performance — in and out, in and out.

The brother in the tree, exasperated, said, "Why don't you stay in there? Then the bull will get tired, go away and we can go home?"

Grandpa replied with vigor, "That's all right for you to say that, sitting up there safe on that limb; but what you don't know is, there's a bear in that cave."

Another bear story grandpa used to tell was used to illustrate the thought that man, when faced with struggle, needs at least an equal break.

When he was sixteen, while walking in a little forest, he encountered a bear that gave chase. He ran and ran; and as he ran he prayed, "Dear God, help me, help me, I need help; and if you won't help me, please, please, don't help that bear."

***

"It's better to face an actual problem than to fret over an imaginary one," suggested this sagacious man of the people.

In calling on a mocker who never darkened the door of the church, grandpa was met with these words: "Well, parson, I've got a problem. It wouldn't be comfortable for me in heaven. How would I get my shirt on over my wings?"

"You have a problem," answered grandpa, "but it's not what you think. It's not about your shirt and heaven. Unless you get started going to church your problem is going to be how to get your hat on over your horns."

"Praising a man will often do more than censuring him," reasoned grandpa. Some church officials in another locality came to him for advice. They said that their preacher had become dull and uninteresting, and that they would like to get rid of him but did not know the best way.

"I'll tell you what to do. Just start bragging on him, and he'll preach himself to death," answered grandpa.

The country man of the cloth always took the op-portunity to teach a needed lesson. As an example: The keys on his piano in his home had turned yellow. Natural-ly it was a conversation piece.

"Is it old?"

"No," he insisted, "the elephant smoked too much."

"No matter how hard you try, some people may think you are overpaid," maintained grandpa. He said that a forlorn, repressed man came into his study and asked, "Do you think it is proper for anyone to profit from the mistakes of another?"

"No, I don't," answered grandpa.

Holding out his hand, the fellow continued, "Then you'll return the five dollars I gave you last year for marrying me."

Grandpa could figure out where the fault lay. He liked to fish. On one trip he and a brother in the church were having no luck at all.

"What's wrong? Why can't we catch some?" inquired the other fisherman.

"Beats me," replied grandpa, "but I don't think my worm is trying."

It was grandpa's observation that the covetous person can always find a way to justify his tight fist. He went to see a very wealthy old man living on borrowed time to whom he explained that he might like to make a nice gift to the Lord.

The old fellow responded: "Yep, I'm old, gettin' older ever'day. You're a lot younger. Jest 'magine I'll be seein' the Lord before you do; so I think I'll jest wait and hand it to Him in person."

"The reasons some people give for not doing a thing exceed all imagination," stated grandpa. He headed a drive to raise money to put a fence around the community cemetery. He called on a dry goods merchant and asked for a donation. He refused. And the preacher expressed himself, "Without being too aggressive, why not?"

"Well, I'll tell you," answered the merchant, "those that are in there can't get out, and those that are out don't want in — we don't need it."

"You can't judge man or beast by appearances" — grandpa's philosophy. Needing a horse, he went to First Monday Trades Day to buy one. A slick horse trader thought he could unload on the preacher; so he trotted a sleek but wind-broken one around for his inspection and by then the nag was panting hard. The owner stroked the horse's back and suggested, "Hasn't he a lovely coat?"

Grandpa, looking at the heaving flanks of the animal, retorted, "Yeah, I like his coat all right, but I don't like his pants."

Grandpa learned that some people need an interpreter. One Sunday he began his sermon by saying, "My topic today is *The Status Quo.*"

"Wait a moment, preacher," called out a brother, "what do you mean by *Status Quo.*"

"That," answered grandpa, "simply means *the mess we're in?*"

Grandpa believed that he should serve the people; and that to do so, he should mingle with them. This is seen in a conversation he had with a city preacher who asked him, "What time do you go to work?"

"Brother, I don't go to work. I'm surrounded with it," replied this country preacher.

"When there is a surplus of anything, there is always the question of what to do with it," stated grandpa. After returning from a revival in a hillbilly community, he was asked about the state of those people. In a thoughtful mood, he slowly answered: "From what I could see and smell, I would say — they live on what they raise and drink the surplus."

"Some things are susceptible to suspicion," contended grandpa. At a wedding rehearsal, the fortunate lady, flashing her diamond, said, "Parson, who originated the custom of the man's giving the woman a diamond engagement ring?"

"I don't know, but I suspect it was a woman," replied the preacher.

Grandpa warned that you should be careful about doing things without the consent of the interested parties. This is seen in the drama in which some local jesters decided to out-banter him.

One night they dragged a dead mule onto the parsonage lawn and left it. Bright and early the next morning, they gathered with others in a little store and telephoned him. The spokesman said, "Parson, I believe it is the duty of you ministers to take care of the dead, and I noticed a dead mule in your yard. Are you going to bury him?"

"Yes, if you'll give your consent," replied the parson.

"Why do I have to give my consent?" inquired the joker.

"Because I have to have the consent of the closest relative," insisted grandpa.

**Grandpa thought a text was something to stick with —
not depart from.** After another preacher had filled the
pulpit, he asked grandpa, "What did you think of my
sermon this morning?"

He replied, "My dear brother, if your text had had
the smallpox, your sermon never could have caught it."

"Even roosters can crow," was another of grandpa's truisms. Two preachers had dinner with him in his home, and they cleaned up the platter of two young roosters. After eating, the preachers walked out into the yard, and an old rooster flew up on the fence and began to crow. One of the ministers commented, "Your rooster is crowing like he's got something to be proud of."

"He has; two of his sons just entered the ministry," retorted grandpa.

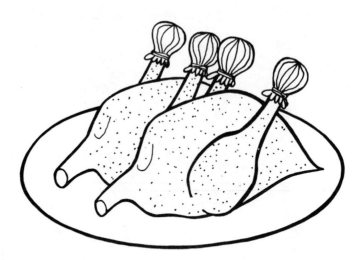